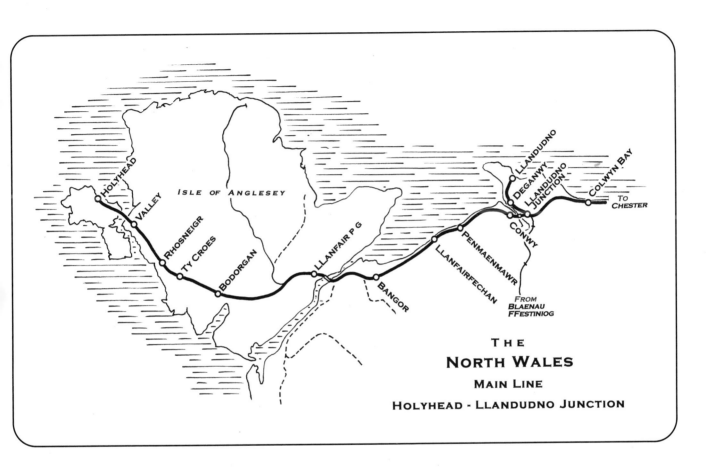

# THE

## NORTH WALES

### Main Line

#### HOLYHEAD - LLANDUDNO JUNCTION

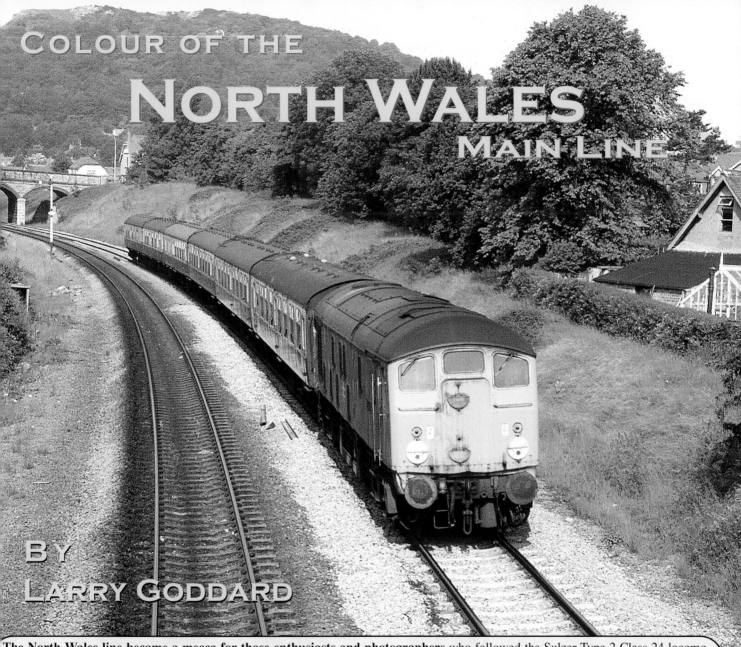

# Colour of the
# North Wales
## Main Line

### By
### Larry Goddard

**The North Wales line became a mecca for those enthusiasts and photographers** who followed the Sulzer Type 2 Class 24 locomotives when, commencing 8 June 1978, several DMU workings were replaced by loco-hauled stock. The rundown of the Class 24 fleet began in earnest in the mid 1970s, and few people expected to see the survivors on passenger duties at this late date. No **24023** approaches Colwyn Bay with the 09.42 Llandudno-Manchester Victoria service on 12 July 1978.

*Olympus    OM1*          *50mm    Zuiko*          *Ektachrome    200*          *1/500, f8*

PUBLISHED BY FOXLINE LIMITED
P O BOX 84, BREDBURY, STOCKPORT. SK6 3YD

PRINTED BY
THE AMADEUS PRESS
CLECKHEATON, WEST YORKSHIRE

**Above:** LMS 'Black Five' No **45407** and Class 47 No. **47849** *Cadeirlan Bangor Cathedral*, leaving Llandudno Junction with 'Y Ddraig Gymreig' special from Holyhead, in celebration of the 150th anniversary of Britannia Bridge on 18 March 2000.

*Nikon F90X      50mm      Kodak Elite 100 Extra      1/250,f4*

# THE NORTH WALES MAIN LINE

## INTRODUCTION

It was the day when the old Chester & Holyhead celebrated its past and future, when technology met tradition, a day when, amid speeches and ceremonies, the public was introduced to trains that would revitalise passenger services from Holyhead, to Chester and beyond, and replace traditional loco-hauled trains. On 18 March 2000, 'Black Five' 4-6-0 No **45407** and Class 47 No **47849** *Cadeirlan Bangor Cathedral*, worked a train from Anglesey to the Welsh mainland, and crossed Robert Stephenson's Britannia Bridge almost 150 years to the minute since the first public train made the crossing in 1850. Although the C&HR opened in 1848, it was another two years before the bridge over the Menai Straits was completed, thus completing a line of railway from London to Holyhead. Early promoters expected traffic to and from the port to be enormous and very little was expected from intermediate traffic, however, it was the growth of the seaside holiday resorts of

**Above:** The present Holyhead station was opened on 17 June 1880 by HRH the Prince of Wales (later King Edward VII). Class 31 No **31418** *Boadicea*, stands in No.1 departure platform, with its Euston type overall roof, after arriving with the 5D03 12.16 Crewe South Yard Royal Mail train on 11 February 1991. Equipment installed in the 1960/70s for the handling of Freightliner containers can be seen in the background, just weeks before closure of the terminal on 18 March.
*Nikon FG    50mm Nikkor    Kodachrome 64    1/250, f4*

Prestatyn, Rhyl, Colwyn Bay and Llandudno that eventually made the old Chester & Holyhead one of the busiest holiday lines in Britain. My own acquaintance with the line began in 1950. Our annual holidays were spent at my grandparents caravan situated beside the busy four-track mainline near Abergele & Pensarn station. Doubtless I was more pleased about this than my parents who complained bitterly about the mini-earthquakes that accompanied each passing train! By the time Abergele became my home in 1965, the character of the line and the towns it served had changed, and the ubiquitous Diesel multiple Unit was beginning to rule supreme – even on services for which it was never designed. Fortunately, the late 1970s heralded a new era of loco-haulage, which has lasted to the present day, and the intention of this album is to show how things were on a day-to-day basis, with the emphasis on the 1970s and 80s. I would like to thank Greg Fox at Foxline for allowing me complete freedom of choice of material and layout, and my fellow photographers who have been kind enough to loan me pictures from their collections. In conclusion, I would like to thank my wife and business partner Mary who, as ever, has given great encouragement. Photographs not credited are the work of the compiler.

LARRY GODDARD, ABERGELE, JANUARY 2002

No **47471** *Norman Tunna GC*, draws its train through the washing plant, past Holyhead station pilot No **08743**, prior to forming the 16.16 to London Euston on 11 February 1991. Alongside is platform3, the main arrival platform, which lost its overall roof in the 1970s during rebuilding of the station.

*Nikon FG        85mm Nikkor        Kodachrome 64        1/250, f5.6*

**HOLYHEAD**

**Unlike today**, three Class 08 Shunters were to be found allocated to Holyhead in the late 1970s. Showing the power of these versatile machines, **08 907** climbs the I in 93 gradient out of the station while shunting stock on the morning of 27 June 1979.                    *Garry Stroud*
*Praktica IV          50mm          Kodachrome 64*

**The North Wales line** was renown as a Class 40 route for over 20 years. Having just taken on fuel, **40099** soaks up the sun while awaiting its next turn of duty on the Wednesday morning of 27 June 1979. The former 4-road steam shed seen in the background, is still a hive of activity at this date. To generations of steam enthusiasts, it was simply '7C' or '6J' depending on ones age.

*Garry Stroud*
*Praktica IV          50mm          Kodachrome 64*

**By the 1990s, the scene has changed somewhat.** Holyhead still has a fuelling point, the old steam shed is gone, and locomotives quite new to the line have all-but taken over all loco-hauled passenger trains. Class 37/4s commenced working a new hourly service in May 1993, and **37408** *Loch Rannoch* is one of a pool of 37s allocated to Crewe for the purpose, pictured switching its train into platform 2 to form the 14.30 to Crewe on 4 September 1993.

*Pentax SP1000*      *55mm Takumar*      *Kodachrome 64*      *1/250, f6.3*

## VALLEY

**Class 40 No 40014**, minus its cast nameplates, passing Valley with a Manchester Victoria-Holyhead service, on 24 August 1978. The local station had closed in 1966 but would reopen in the early 80s. A Triangle for turning steam locomotives would be laid in Valley goods yard in 1989. This yard is also the collection point for Nuclear Flasks. Delivered by road from Wylfa Power Station, they are taken by rail for reprocessing.

*Garry    Stroud            Praktica    IV            50mm            Kodachrome    64*

7

**This picture, taken almost 20 years to the day** after the picture on the previous page, shows one of the scenic delights of Anglesey, Rhosneigr Lake. Class 37 No **37426** wheels the 13.54 Holyhead-Birmingham New Street southwards on a hot 27 August 1998. Rhosneigr station opened in May 1907, although the present day buildings date from 1953.

*Nikon F301        50mm Nikkor        Fujichrome Velvia        1/250,  f5.6*

RHOSNEIGR

# TY CROES

**Ty Croes Station** is just short of 3 miles from Rhosneigr and has staggered platforms, either side of a level crossing. Class 37 No. **37414** *Cathays C&W Works 1846-1993*, working the 12.20 Crewe Holyhead service, on 16 August 1997, passes the very unusual signal box, integral with a Booking Office and Waiting Room.

*EOS-600*     *Kodak   Elite   100*     *1/1000,   f4*

**It is a case of back to the future** for the lovely station at Bodorgan, after its Francis Thompson cottage style buildings had stood derelict and roofless for many years. In the 1990s, the new owner has not only rebuilt the buildings and platform canopy, he also repainted the station in early BR colours of crimson and cream. The station makes a fine setting for 1960s liveried Class 101 DMU No **101 685** as it picks up passengers while working the 12.20 Holyhead-Llandudno local stopping train on 11 February 2000. Note the slate slab name tablet set into the wall.

*Canon      EOS-5*                    *50mm    Canon*                          *Fujichrome      100*                    *1/250,    f5.6*

## MALLTRAETH

Class 37 No **37408** *Loch Rannoch*, whisks the 10.07 Birmingham New Street-Holyhead over the gracefully arched viaduct at Malltraeth on 20 May 1999. By this date, the celebrity loco has exchanged its British Railways large-logo livery for the colours of English, Welsh & Scottish Railway.

*Pentax 645      75mm Takumar      Fujichrome 100      1/1000,f4*

**The comparative flatness of Anglesey compared with the mountainous Welsh mainland** can be seen in this picture of Class 40 No **40015** *Aquitania*, racing across the island towards Llanfair P,G, with the 12/48 Holyhead-Euston on Friday, 25 August 1978. The station at Llanfair PG was originally the eastern terminus of the line from Holyhead until Britannia Bridge was completed over the Menai Straits. Having closed in February 1966 under the Beeching proposals, Llanfair would re-open on a temporary basis on the 29th May 1970 following damage to the Brittannia Bridge. Following reinstatement of the link with the mainland, Llanfair once again was subjected to closure *(31.1.1972)* only for public pressure to force a permanent return to the network on 7th May 1973.

*Garry Stroud*                    *Praktica IV*                    *50mm*                    *Kodachrome64*

**Britannia Bridge, spanning the Menai Straits**, was the final link in the Chester & Holyhead railway and opened in 1850. The present steel-arch structure replaced the original tubular bridge after the latter was burned down in 1970. Just visible on the bridge is Class 37 No **37415**, working the 13.23 Holyhead to Manchester Piccadilly service on 30 March 2000. The next station between here and Bangor was Menai Bridge *(closed 14.2.1966)*, which had at one time served as a junction for the branch to Carnaerfon.

*Canon EOS-5    35mm    Kodak Elite 100 Extra    1/500, f4.5*

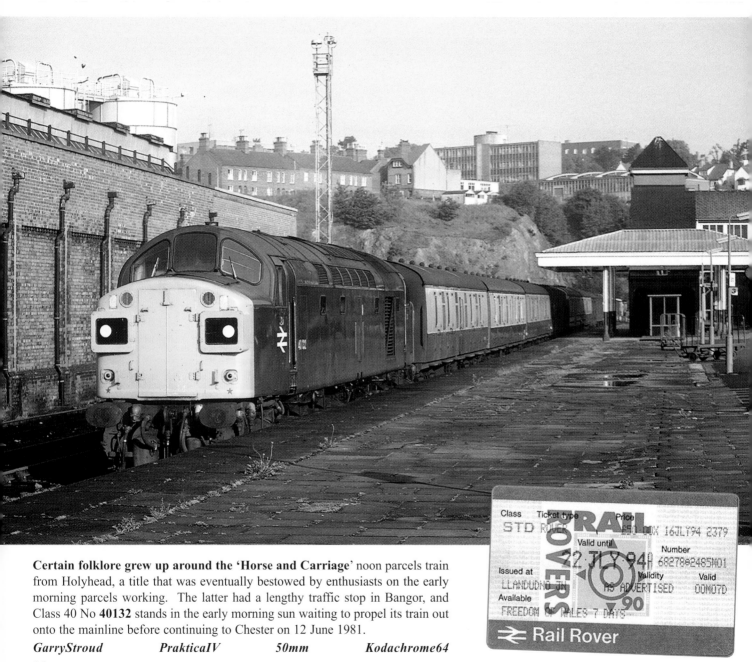

**Certain folklore grew up around the 'Horse and Carriage'** noon parcels train from Holyhead, a title that was eventually bestowed by enthusiasts on the early morning parcels working. The latter had a lengthy traffic stop in Bangor, and Class 40 No **40132** stands in the early morning sun waiting to propel its train out onto the mainline before continuing to Chester on 12 June 1981.

*GarryStroud*          *PrakticaIV*          *50mm*          *Kodachrome64*

## BANGOR

**Despite major remodelling at other stations on the line**, Bangor manages to remain quite intact, and this view will look familiar to visitors today, except of course for the motive power! On 7 June 1982, No **40124** is on the 13.58 service to Manchester Victoria, while a Gloucester RCW Unit No M56111 and M50356, is working the 12.20 Llandudno-Holyhead local. *Garry Stroud* *Praktica IV 50mm Kodachrome 64*

**At 11.35 on 17 April 1999,** the passing of a Class 101 Unit briefly shatters the small-village solitude of Tal-Y-Bont, as it heads towards its next stop at Bangor. Welcomed in the 1950s as the likely saviour of branch line services, the Metro-Cammell DMUs have been around for over 45 years, no doubt due to their strong and uncomplicated design.
*Nikon F90X     70-200HSM Sigma zoom     Kodak ExtraColour 100     1/250, ƒ5.6*

'HERITAGE'
UNITS

## THE 'GREEN MACHINE'

**The illustrious machines of the steam-era** are a hard act to follow, but fortunately for railfans, the diesel era has produced some very impressive machines, amongst them the English Electric Type 4. As the last member of the class left in green livery, having been given a fresh coat of green at its classified repair in 1978, **40106** enter Llanfairfechan with the 11.30 Bangor-Manchester Victoria on 24 August 1979.
*Nikon FM     50mm Nikkor          Ektachrome  200          1/250,f5.6*

**The Chester & Holyhead line is synonymous with 'The Irish Mail'**, which was the preserve of 'Royal Scot' locomotives and latterly 'Britannia' Pacific's in the steam era. No **70000** *Britannia*, complete with an appropriate headboard, evokes memories of a past era as it storms through Llanfairfechan on 5 July 1992. Preserved steam has polished the rails to North Wales since 1989.

*Nikon F601      70-210 APO Sigma zoom      Ektachrome 100      1/500, f4.5*

THE 'IRISH MAIL'

# LLANFAIRFECHAN

**Class 37s** appeared on Cardiff-Rhyl trains in 1988/9, at a time when the class was rarely seen on the North Wales line, but this process accelerated in 1993 as Regional Railways sought to replace the ageing Class 31s on its Crewe-Manchester trains. **37414** *Cathays C&W Works 1846-1993*, speeds along the promenade at Llanfairfechan with the 14.23 Birmingham-Holyhead on 28 July 1999. ***Nikon F90X      35mm Nikkor      Fujichrome 100      1/500, ƒ5.6***

**Beyond Llanfairfechan the railway encounters the headland of Penmaenmawr.** Owing to quarrying operations the railway has been built as close to the sea as possible and is carried over a short sea viaduct, an unusual feature and the 231 yards long Pen-y-Clip Tunnel pierces the headland itself. An unidentified Class 37 is working the 17.17 Crewe-Bangor across the structure on 24 August 1998. The A55 road viaduct, built in the 1930s, can be seen higher up the towering mountain.

*Nikon F301*          *35mm*          *Fujichrome Velvia*          *1/125, f2.8*

PEN-Y-CLIP

# PENMAENMAWR

**A 1958-built Derby 2-car DMU**, No M50927 and M56361, enters Penmaenmawr station with the 16.10 Llandudno Junction to Bangor local service on 25 June 1979. Track ballast has been produced at nearby quarries since around 1888. Ballast trains from the 'down' direction could only gain access to the quarry yard by drawing into the station, before setting back over the 'up' line into a headshunt. Direct access to the yard from the 'down' line would become possible in the 1980s following reconstruction of the yard in connection with the building of the new A55 road.

*Garry Stroud*
*Praktica IV   50mm   Kodachrome 64*

BRITISH RAILWAYS BOARD (M) **82** 2nd CLASS WEEKLY SEASON TICKET Rate £1.18.0

VALID UNTIL

**2 4 JAN 70**

BETWEEN **COLWYN BAY**

AND **BANGOR**

Signature of holder *R. S. Cutler*
FOR CONDITIONS ENQUIRE AT TICKET OFFICE

This Ticket is NOT TRANSFERABLE and must be given up on expiry   № 6389

**Class 40 No 40135 stands in the yard at Penmaenmawr** as its train of empties begins the process of becoming a loaded ballast train on 22 February 1986. Taken out of storage for the remodelling of Crewe Station, the loco is renumbered 97406, but to most enthusiasts it is still 40135! Despite cracks in its bogies, the loco would soldier on for another nine months before final withdrawal.

*Olympus   OM1*          *100mm   Zuiko*          *Kodahcrome   64*          *1/125.f6.3*

BALLAST
WORKINGS

# PENMAENMAWR

**The new congregation in Penmaenmawr yard** on 20 May 1986 includes No **31286** drawing its loaded wagons away from the hopper, and No **25278**, which has just arrived with empties. This is one of the first appearances of a Class 31 in the yard, soon to take over most ballast workings, but for 25278 and her sisters the future is not nearly so bright.

*Nikon FG*        *50mm*        *Kodachrome 64*        *1/125,f6.3*

**(Above) The sea wall at Penmaenmawr** with No **47546** heading the 15.45 Manchester-Bangor past the gas works on 3 May 1983. Visible in the distance is the old footbridge, known to local train fans as *'the iron bridge'*. It would be swept away along with the gas works by the new A55 road, nevertheless, the new bridge would continue to carry the old title….. such is the power of tradition!                                            *Garry Stroud*
*Pentax ME-Super       80-200 zoom       Kodachrome 64*

**(Right) Begrimed but not disgraced**, un-rebuilt No **37131** finds itself on prestige passenger assignment hauling Virgin Train's 08.50 Holyhead-Euston, and keeping good time as it approaches Penmaenbach on 18 July 1998. No doubt word has spread down the enthusiast grapevine and has helped to increase passenger-numbers in the process.

*Pentax 6 x 7     105mm Takumar     Fujichrome Velvia     1/500,f4*

**(Left) Passing the site of a long-departed Military training camp,** Dutch liveried Class 37/0 No **37106**, cuts between Bryn Morfa holiday camp and Conwy football ground with new EWS wagons destined for Warrington on 16 July 1997.
*Pentax 6 x 7    105mm Takumar    Fujichrome Velvia    1/500, f4*

**(Above)  Railfreight liveried Class 31** No **31201** exits the tunnel at Conwy with a Nuclear Flask train from Wylfa en route to Sellafield on 1 July 1987.  The train would shortly pass through the new Conwy Station, which opened a few days earlier on 27 June.
*Nikon FG    50mm Nikkor    Kodachrome 64    1/250, f2.8*

(Above) **Class 20s** No **20104** and **20090**, resplendent in new Railfreight colours, head a Springs Branch to Penmaenmawr Quarry working through Conwy Arch and on past the site of the original Conway Station on 25 July 1985.

*Olympus OM1 35-70 Zuiko zoom      Kodachrome 64      1/250, f4*

THROUGH THE CASTLE WALLS

# CONWY

**The ancient walls of Conwy Castle** keep watch over No **47366** *Institute of Civil Engineers* as it comes off the tubular bridge with a block train of empty 'Tiger' wagons from Ashburys on 28 April 1988. This train is made up of 29 POA wagons built on the chassis of ex-45 ton tank wagons. After loading at Penmaenmawr quarry, it will return to Ashburys with 1,334 tonnes of granite chippings for distribution in the Manchester area.

*Contax   139   Quartz*          *50mm*          *Kodachrome   64*          *1/250,   f5.6*

**Above: A delightful view of Llandudno Junction** crossing, looking from the Llandudno branch towards Llandudno Junction. The old steam-era track layout is sharply defined by a fresh coating of snow. A Class 101 is heading for Holyhead with an all-stations working from Llandudno on 27 January 1979. The carriage shed can be seen on the right of the picture where minor servicing of locomotives takes place. It would remain a fuelling point until circa 1986. *Larry Davies*     *Canon AE-1*     *50mm Canon*     *Kodachrome 64*

# THE LLANDUDNO BRANCH

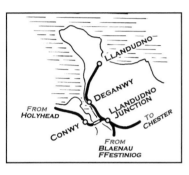

**Only a handful of Class 24 locos remain in traffic by 1978**, usually working light duties, but in a surprise move some of the survivors have been put on DMU-replacement services working from Bangor and Llandudno to Crewe and Manchester Victoria. No **24023** takes the Llandudno line out of Llandudno Junction with the 13.30 from Manchester on 12 July 1978.

*Olympus OM1      100mm Zuiko*
*Ektachrome 200      1/500,  f8*

**Left: Posed in the rising sun at Llandudno**, three class 40s stand at the head of their respective trains after arriving with empty-stock for Saturday's early morning departures. No **40112** will work the 09.42 to Manchester, while **40118** will depart for London Euston. No **40025**, nearest the camera, waits for customers before heading off to Yorkshire with the 09.00 to York, 24 August 1979.

*Larry Davies*
*Canon AE1   50mm Canon   Agfachrome.*

# LLANDUDNO

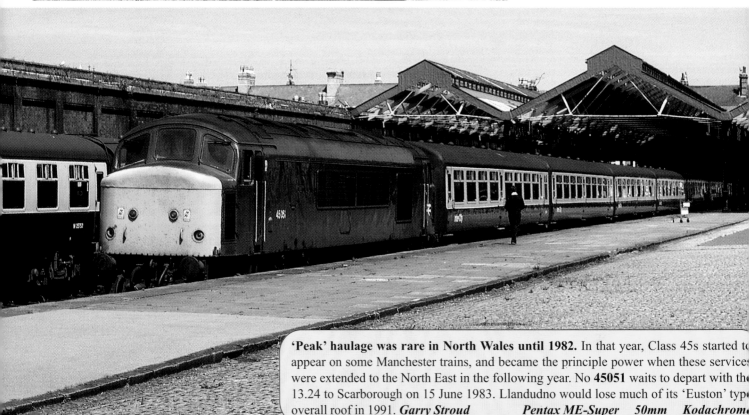

**'Peak' haulage was rare in North Wales until 1982.** In that year, Class 45s started to appear on some Manchester trains, and became the principle power when these services were extended to the North East in the following year. No **45051** waits to depart with the 13.24 to Scarborough on 15 June 1983. Llandudno would lose much of its 'Euston' type overall roof in 1991. *Garry Stroud*                   *Pentax ME-Super   50mm   Kodachrome*

**In addition to frequent excursions to Skegness**, Class 20s put in appearances at Llandudno in the 1990s on the weekdays 08.11 from Derby. No **20007** and **20032** are stepping out of the terminus at Llandudno, past No 2 signal box, on the start of their journey back to Derby at 17.14hrs on 28 June 1991.  Despite the fact that Llandudno is a Mecca for holidaymakers, the station would have few facilities on offer by the end of the century. *Nikon FG     85mm Nikkor     Fujichrome 100     1/250, f5.6*

**The North Wales line was used to test refurbished Class 37s** as they were out-shopped from Crewe Works, sometimes at the head of timetabled trains, and some-times on special test trains composed of redundant coaching stock. No **37503**, heads a test train through Deganwy on 21 February 1986. This loco would return to north Wales seven years later while based in the Trainload Freight West pool at Crewe.

*Olympus OM1        100mm Zuiko        Ektachrome 100        1/250, f5.6*

# DEGANWY

**Back at Llandudno Junction,** 'Peak' No **45117** has just arrived in platform 2 with the 08.20 Newcastle-Llandudno on 6 September 1985. Despite its smart appearance, 45117 would be withdrawn 9 months later in May 1986.

*Pentax SP1000 105mm Tamron*
*Kodachrome 64     1/125, f8*

# L L A N D U D N O
# J U N C T I O N
# T O
# C H E S T E R

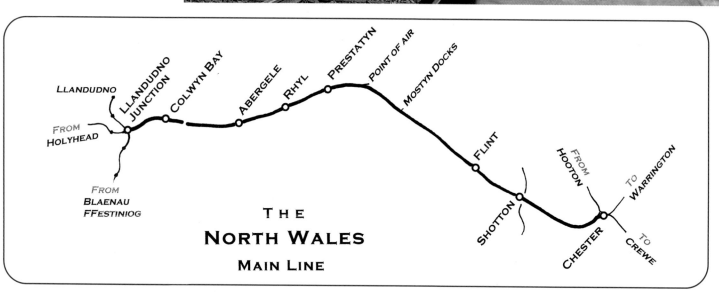

LLANDUDNO

FROM HOLYHEAD

LLANDUDNO JUNCTION

COLWYN BAY

ABERGELE

RHYL

PRESTATYN

POINT OF AIR

MOSTYN DOCKS

FLINT

FROM HOOTON

TO WARRINGTON

SHOTTON

CHESTER

TO CREWE

FROM BLAENAU FFESTINIOG

# THE
# NORTH WALES
## MAIN LINE

**Class 56 locos commenced working to Llandudno Junction on 28 September 1982**, hauling fly ash from Fiddlers Ferry in connection with the construction of the A55 'Expressway'. No **56087** rides high over the temporary unloading facility situated behind the loco depot on 5 September 1983. Extra sidings were laid in Junction yard to store these trains while wagon doors are checked over after unloading is completed. *Philip Hindley*

*Nikon FE*                                    *50mm Nikkor*                                    *Kodachrome 64*

SHORT-LIVED
FLY ASH
FACILITY

**DESTINATION**

**MANCHESTER**

**Llandudno Junction from the east,** with Class 25 No **25212** departing with the 11.30 Bangor-Manchester Victoria on 18 August 1978. The track leading in from bottom-left is the Conway Valley branch. The DMU refurbishment program and the blue asbestos factor have led to a shortage of Units, hence the loco hauled train.

*Olympus OM1*      *50mm Zuiko*      *Ektachrome 200*      *1/500, f8*

37

**A comparison with the previous picture** shows that trackwork at the east end of the station has actually increased. The 'up' slow line is re-instated as far as Conwy Corner and there is a new junction with the Conwy Valley Branch, while the old track serves as a long siding giving access to Glan Conwy yard opened in 1980 to replace the yard at Colwyn Bay. No **47520** speeds through the station with the 12.45 Holyhead-Euston relief boat train on 19 June 1988.

*Mamiya 645    110mm Secor C    Fujichrome 100    1/500, f4.5*

**During the mid 1980s the owners of Penmaenmawr quarry** entered into a contract with Peakstone to supply limestone to Hope Street, Manchester. Using 21 RMC Roadstone bogie wagons, this Fridays-only train commenced on 20 March 1987 using mainly Class 37/6 locos. No **37679** and **37680** pass under Queens Road Bridge on the approach to Llandudno Junction with 'Down' empties on 6 May 1988.

*Contax    139    Quartz        50mm        Kodachrome    64        1/250.    f4*

**In 1963, a connection was laid between the LNWR line and the GWR line at Blaenau Ffestiniog** to facilitate the removal of Nuclear waste from the power station at Trawsfynydd via the Conwy Valley branch. No **25035** leaves the branch at Llandudno Junction with a flask train on 13 June 1986. It would be a regular Sulzer Type 2 turn until 1987.

*Nikon FG     105mm Tamron     Kodachrome 25     1/250, f4*

OFF THE
CONWY VALLEY
BRANCH

## SUMMER SATURDAY

**A typical summer Saturday of the period** with no less than eight Class 40s working trains down the coast, including: 40022, 40031, 40108, 40079, 40067, 40009, and 40093. No **40092** approaches Llandudno Junction with the 09.29 Manchester Victoria-Llandudno on 19 August 1978… happy days.

*Olympus OM1     45-150 Soligor zoom     Ektachrome 200     1/500, f8*

**Having run block to block behind a passenger train all the way from Chester**, No **40057** climbs away from a signal check at Colwyn Bay with the 14.54 Trafford Park to Holyhead FLT on the evening of 15 July 1980,. The truncated track on the right is in use as a head-shunt for trains entering the low-level yard at Colwyn Bay, although at one time it was part of the 'down' slow line between Colwyn Bay and Llandudno Junction put in at the turn of the 20th Century.

*Olympus OM1    100mm Zuiko    Kodachrome 64    1/250, f4*

## 'WHISTLERS' IN NORTH WALES

**Class 40 No 40141 coasts down grade towards Colwyn Bay** with a rake of BR Mk.I corridor and open stock forming the 10.40 Llandudno-Manchester Victoria on 23 May 1980. Present day visitors to this spot may be disappointed to find that the railway has been realigned; the foreground is now occupied by the A55 'Expressway'.

*Pentax MX        70-150 Tamron zoom        Kodachrome 64        1/250, f4*

**Colwyn Bay Goods Yard is on a much lower level than the mainlin**e, built in a pit that resulted from construction of the embankment in the area. The yard is entered down a gradient and through a tunnel under the station forecourt. An unidentified Class 25 stands waiting to leave the yard in the spring sunshine after dropping off wagons of coal and oil in March 1976. *Philip Hindley*              *Canon Canonette    Kodachrome 64*

COLWYN BAY
GOODS

**Class 45 'Peak' No 45145 is rostered for the 11.15 Bangor-Newcastle service on 20 May 198**4, and restarts the train from the scheduled Colwyn Bay stop. The station overlooks the promenade and is somewhat exposed to the elements, hence the familiar LNWR semi-glass screen seen to the right of the train. Having survived similar screens at Rhyl and Llandudno Junction, it would be demolished in February 2000.    *Mamiya 645    150mm Secor C    Ektachrome 100*

**Colwyn Bay station is a relatively modern erection of 1907**, having 'Up' and 'Down'
island platforms, so that fast could pass stopping trains if required. Class 47 No **47450** has
priority through platform one with the 15.03 Holyhead-Euston while Class 25 No **25327**
sits it out in platform two with a Freightliner from Holyhead on 26 August 1980.

*Philip Hindley*                    *Nikon FE    50mm Nikkor    Kodachrome 64*

COLWYN
BAY

## OLD COLWYN

**Class 37 No 37518, overtakes road traffic on the adjacent A55** as it gets into its stride hauling the Sundays-only 09.28 Holyhead-Crewe on 8 September 1996. The train is passing the site of Old Colwyn station, which lost its passenger facilities in 1952. One small trace of the station that survives to this day is the subway leading to the promenade.

*Canon T70    200mm Canon    Fujichrome 100    1/500, f5.6*

**Class 40 No 40013** *Andania* **climbs to Penmaenrhos Tunnel** with the 17.42 Manchester Victoria to Llandudno Junction on 30 July 1981. This is the site of Llysfaen station that closed in 1931 although Llysfaen signal box is destined to survive until 15 December 1983.

*Mamiya 645     150mm Secor C     Ektachrome 200     1/500, f8*

LLYSFAEN

# Engineering
## Work

**The decision to reinstate Class 40 No 40122/D200** to service in its original livery in 1983 helped to attract considerable extra revenue wherever it worked passenger trains, however, it is seen on more mundane duty working a permanent way train through Llysfaen on 11 September 1986. The 648yd Penmaenrhos Tunnel is visible in the background.

*Nikon FG        105mm Tamron        Kodachrome 64        1/500, ƒ4.5*

**Class 45 No 45007 makes light work of lifting a train** of welded rails up the 1-in-100 Llandulas incline on 26 June 1985. The pathway to the right of the train once carried sidings that were built on level ground in the aftermath of the Abergele accident of 1868. Four loaded wagons of paraffin were shunted against a brake van, which was standing on the mainline with its brakes applied. Shortly after the shunt, all five wagons were seen moving down the incline 'wrong line'. They collided with the 'Irish Mail' near Abergele.

*Nikon FG     105mm Nikkor     Kodachrome 64     1/500,f4*

# LLANDULAS

**The early bird catches the worm** and, in this instance, the passage of Class 37 No **37415** working the 06.35 Holyhead-Birmingham New Street across Llandulas Viaduct on a hot 29 July 1999.

*Nikon F90X     35mm Nikkor     Fujichrome 100     1/500, f5.6*

**Class 20 No 20110 leads another member of the class over the River Dulas** while working the 14.55 Penmaenmawr to Bamber Bridge ballast on 7 August 1989. This trifling watercourse has a history of causing much damage when swollen and in 1879 it undermined and washed away the original stone viaduct. The present structure was built and in operation within 8 days of the mishap – a record by any standards. It received a new concrete deck in the 1970s.

*Pentax SP1000     50mm     Kodachrome 64     1/500, f3.5*

**Class 47 No 47231** *The Silcock Express*, climbs away from Abergele with a special 'Down' Speedlink service on 17 May 1988. This is the site of the Abergele accident of 1868, in which drums of paraffin, almost eight tons of it, were thrown from runaway wagons as they collided head on with the down 'Irish Mail' and engulfed the engine and leading four coaches in a gigantic fireball. 32 victims of the accident are buried in the churchyard at Abergele.

*Mamiya 645     110mm Secor C     Ektachrome 100     1/1000, f3.5*

**Photographed from Llandulas Mountain**, Class 40 No **40150** *Crewe*, with its name neatly painted on each side, rolls down the grade between Llysfaen and Abergele with the 7F18 Associated Octel tanks from Amlwch to Ellesmere Port on 29 June 1984. From Abergele, the line is relatively flat as far as Chester.
*Mamiya 645          150mm Secor C          Ektachrome 200          1/250, f9.3*

AMLWCH TANKS
EN-ROUTE

**The London &North Western Railway was fond of tall repeater signals** of which the North Wales line had its fare share at one time. The one guarding the west end of Abergele & Pensarn station has just pulled off to allow Class 40 No **40173** to start the steady climb to Llysfaen with its Holyhead-bound Freightliner train on a warm August evening in 1976. *Olympus OM1    50mm Zuiko    Agfachrome CT18*

# HOLYHEAD BOUND

ABERGELE

**An interest in just one type of locomotive was rare in steam days**, but Diesel fans seem to live quite comfortably with monomania. This may be the reason why the 'Peaks' were slow to gain acceptance from the local enthusiasts still mourning the demise of the Class 40s. The 'Peaks', impressive in looks and performance, won everyone over in the end. No **45016** speeds through Abergele with the 06.30 Holyhead-Willesden Freightliner train on Wednesday 24 April 1985. *Nikon FG    85mm Nikkor    Kodachrome 64    1/500, f4*

**Straight out of the box!** Brand new Class 56 No **56132**, on test from Crewe Works, leads an unidentified Class 47 through Abergele with the 09.30 Crewe-Holyhead on 23 May 1984. The neat building on the 'Up' platform is one of the original Thompson buildings of 1848 which, having survived the quadrupling of tracks in 1902 when much of the station was rebuilt, but would succumb to the economies of the 1980s in November 1986.

*Mamiya 645    150mm Secor C    Ektachrome 200    1/500, f5.6*

**It is a typically busy Easter Monday of the 1970s** with Bank Holiday trains arriving at Rhyl at: 10.02 from Rock Ferry, 10.13 from Liverpool, 10.24 from Stoke, 10.33 from Lichfield, 10.44 from Manchester, 10.52 from Wolverhampton, 11.02 from Barrow, 11.14 from Buxton, 12.02 from Manchester Oxford Road, 12.12 from Coventry, 13.18 relief from Euston, and 13.45 from Euston. Class 40 No **40015** *Aquitania* passes Foryd Junction, one time connection with the Vale of Clwyd line to Denbigh, with the 11.02 Barrow-Llandudno on 27 March 1978. *Mamiya 645  150mm Secor C  Agfachrome  1/250, f8*

## SCOTRAIL ON TEST

**Newly overhauled push-pull Scotrail Class 47 No 47709** *The Lord Provost* pilots **47441** away from Rhyl with the 09.30 Euston-Holyhead on 11 March 1987. The truncated track on the right is all that remains of the one-time slow line that remained in use as far as Abergele until 1972.

*Nikon FG     50mm Nikkor     Kodachrome 64     1/500, f4*

**No 47447 hustles the 06.13 Holyhead-Trafford Park Freightliner** through the "H" bridge at Rhyl on 1 July 1986. British Rail chose the port of Holyhead for its Freightliner operations, as it offered shorter sea-passages to Belfast as well as Dublin than either Liverpool or Heysham. The financial footing of the North Wales line would suffer a major blow in 1991 with the abrupt closure of the Holyhead Freightliner terminal.

*Nikon FG*      *105mm Tamron*      *Kodachrome 64*      *1/250, f6.3*

**RHYL**

**Thursday 31 May 1984 finds Class 25 No 25161** trundling through Rhyl with the early morning parcels train from Holyhead. A preceding DMU has cleared the up platform of commuters but congestion on the line at this time of morning is such that trains are running block to block and freights are regularly put into the loops at Holywell and Mold Junction before reaching Chester.
*Mamiya 645        150mm Secor C        Ektachrome 200        1/500, f6.3*

**Class 40 No 40030 coasts into Rhyl** with the 15.40 Manchester Victoria to Bangor train on 10 July 1980, passing the out of use carriage shed. Mid-week excursion traffic often terminated at Rhyl and was stored in sidings adjacent to the Down island platform. Remodelling in 1990 would reduce the station's capacity for train-storage.

*Olympus OM1*          *70-150 Tamron zoom*          *Kodachrome 64*          *1/250, f4*

APPROACHING
RHYL

RHYL
PANORAMA

**This view of Rhyl looking towards Chester** shows the large island platform on the 'Down' side. The bays, once used by the Vale of Clwyd trains ot Denbigh, Ruthin and Corwen, are now trackless. No **47105** and **47198** leave the goods yard with ballast for Kinmel Bay, where re-alignment of the 'Up' line is taking place, whilst a Class 25 stands in the yard on two coaches. Another Class 47 waits to leave for the depot at Llandudno Junction on 17 March 1985. *Mamiya 645    150mm Secor C    Ektachrome 200    1/250, f8*

**Class 47 No 47454 steps lively out of Rhyl**, under the semaphore signals at Grange Road, while working the 07.09 Holyhead-Cardiff up 'Welshman' on 7 September 1987. The Tran Pennine coaches were cascaded from other services when Class 150/2 'Sprinters' replaced some loco-hauled services in March 1987. Interestingly, this livery would continue to remain in use, although with other brand names, for many years to come.

*Nikon    FG            50mm    Nikkor            Kodachrome    64            1/500,f4*

**Colourful station gardens were a part of the railway scene for many years**, and competitions were organised in the various districts for the Best Kept Station award. Prestatyn was the winner of the 'Wales in bloom' competition in 1987 with its fine display of flowers laid out in gardens on the down slow platform. Class 47 No **47601** *Glorious Devon*, hurries past on the fast line working the 09.35 Euston-Holyhead on a hot 27 August 1987.

*Nikon FG      50mm Nikkor      Kodachrome 64      1/1000, f2.8*

**As befitting its traffic importance, Prestatyn had platforms on all four tracks until the late 1960s,** although the down slow track continued to play an important role in keeping trains rolling until March 1990. The 08.15 Newcastle-Bangor is pathed to run via the slow line to allow the 10.10 from Euston to overtake it between here and Rhyl. Class 45 No **45133** departs the station on the down slow line on 22 April 1985. *Nikon FG20* *135mm Nikkor* *Kodachrome 64* *1/250, f5.6*

## THE WELSHMAN

**From May 1985, Class 33s added yet more variety to the North Wales motive power scene,** brought in to work a new named service, 'The Welshman', which linked north and south Wales. The 11.15 Crewe-Bangor departs Prestatyn behind ScotRail Class 47 No **47645** and Class 33 No **33027** *Lord Mountbatten of Burma* on 5 May 1986. The Class 47 is on test following refurbishment at Crewe.      *Olympus OM1      100mm Zuiko      Kodachrome 64      1/500, f4.5*

**Flanked by the pleasant greens of late spring,** Class 45 No **45112** *Royal Army Ordnance Corps* glides majestically out of Prestatyn with the 11.15 Bangor-Scarborough on 4 May 1984. The 'Peaks' have managed to maintain an air of dignity in their twilight years unlike the Class 40s with their patched up nose ends and missing grills. *Mamiya 645     150mm Secor C     Ektachrome 64     1/125, f8*

PRESTATYN

**Posters proclaiming 'Space Travel---ETA 12 May 1986' had announced the imminent 'Sprinterisation' of the North Wales line.** Within a matter of weeks, the new Class 150/1 'Sprinters' and Class 142 'Pacers' were working services to Manchester, Blaenau Ffestiniog and Crewe, as well as local services to Holyhead. Within a year the newer Class 150/2 units began making inroads into Trans-Pennine services, the route of the Class 45s. Nos **150 230, 150 230** and **150 222** depart Prestatyn with the 10.53 Scarborough-Holyhead on 16 March 1987, the first day of Sprinter-operation. The grey ends would shortly be given a coat of yellow paint.

*Nikon FG     105mm Nikkor     Kodachrome 64     1/250,f5.6*

**One of the staple freight flows on the North Wales line for many years** was the shipment of sulphur from Mostyn Dock to the Associated Octel plant at Amlwch, on the Isle of Anglesey. An Amlwch-bound working passes Gronant behind Class 47 No **47379** *Total Energy*, on 13 April 1988. Sulphur is a messy traffic, and the vacuum-braked HKV wagons are always sheeted over before leaving Mostyn Dock. The final shipment would take place on 17 May 1989. ***Contax 139 Quartz    100mm    Kodachrome 64    1/125, f8***

## TALACRE

**Another well-known freight flow is the Humber Oil Refinery – Holyhead**, conveying import-ed petroleum coke to the Rio Tinto Zinc plant. Class 47 No **47223** passes the remains of Talacre Station with the return empties on 20 October 1988. The station served the outer slow lines only until closure in 1966. Since then the 'up' slow line has served as a head shunt for colliery traffic to and from Point of Air. *Mamiya 645   80mm Secor   Ektachrome 100   1/250, f6.*

**Class 20 locomotives regularly worked the MGR traffic** between Point of Air colliery and Fiddlers Ferry Power Station until replaced by more modern motive power in the 90s. Nos **20073** and **20181** propel a train of freshly painted hopper wagons into the colliery complex on 31 October 1988. This is one of the first trains to use the new track layout into the yard, which replaced the old connection provided for the colliery in 1907. *Nikon FG   105mm Nikkor   Kodachrome 64   1/60,*

POINT
OF
AIR

**The Anglesey Aluminium complex near Holyhead** used to generate a fair amount of traffic for the daily 'trip' to Mold Junction and Arpley. This took the form of aluminium billets, loaded in high-capacity Cargowaggons. The train called at Bangor for Tunnel Cement empties, and Llandudno Junction private sidings belonging to Heron Oils and National Fuels Distribution, where empty petroleum tanks and coal wagons would be added to the train. On occasions the train would be quite lengthy by the time it departed at around 14.30hrs. An Arpley bound Speedlink passes Mostyn behind Class 47 No **47344** on 28 April 1987.

*Nikon FG   85mm Nikkor   Kodachrome 64     1/500, f4*

**A loaded coal train from Point of Air moves effortlessly through Mostyn** on a bright but chilly 26 November 1991. On this, the second day of Class 60-haulage, No **60071** *Dorothy Garrod* , provides serious horsepower after years of Class 20 haulage. Point of Air colliery traffic would linger on for another five years with the final coal train departing behind 56133 on 17 September 1996. *Nikon FG   50mm Nikkor   Kodak Elite 100   1/500, f4*

# MOSTYN

## DESTINED FOR PRESERVATION

**Battle-scarred Class 40 No 40135** passes Holywell Junction with Penmaenmawr-bound empties on 7 November 1985. This popular machine would enter preservation on the East Lancashire Railway at Bury where it continues to endure.

*Nikon FG     50mm Nikkor     Kodachrome 64     1/500, f2*

**The train is a ballast working but the image is far removed from the days of rail-blue and hopper wagons**. General Motors Class 66 No **66163** presents the face of Britain's leading rail freight operator, English, Welsh & Scottish, as it hauls American-style gondola wagons through the closed station at Holywell Junction on 26 February 2000. The destination for the Railtrack-leased wagons is Guide Bridge. The old slow lines remain in use as passing loops. *Nikon F90X    50mm Nikkor    Fujichrome 100    1/500, f4.*

## 'INDUSTRIAL' NORTH WALES

**The massive Courtaulds factory** dominates the area around Greenfield as Class 47 No **47538** cuts through the complex with the 'Welshman', the 07.05 Holyhead-Cardiff, on 30 June 1986. Sidings into the works were last used in 1985.

*Nikon FG     105mm Tamron     Kodachrome 64     1/500, ƒ5.6*

**An assortment of ex LMS, LNER and GWR Tube wagons** make up most of the composition of this Tunnel Inspection train seen passing Greenfield behind Class 31 No **31144** on 19 March 1987. The train has been in use inspecting the 2 miles 206yds long Ffestiniog Tunnel at the summit of the Conwy Valley line. By this date, much of the Courtaulds factory complex has been flattened. *Nikon FG    50mm Nikkor    Kodachrome 64    1/500, f4*

**GREENFIELD**

## THE FFESTINIOG PULLMAN

**If enthusiast-reception for the 'Peaks' was at first indifferent**, the arrival of the Class 33 'Cromptons' was a different story altogether. No 33008 was the first entrant working 'The Ffestiniog Pullman' as far as Llandudno Junction on 13 June 1982, then the May 1985 summer-timetable brought the class to the Chester-Holyhead line on a regular basis, and drivers soon found the trackside lined with photographers. No **33026** speeds through Bagillt with the 12.00 Cardiff-Llandudno on 18 June 1986      ***Nikon FG      105mm Tamron      Kodachrome 64      1/500, f4***

**A warm summer breeze furrows the waters of the tidal basin at Bagillt** as Class 37/4 No **37418** *East Lancashire Railway*, cruises across marshland towards Chester with the 13.54 Holyhead-Birmingham New Street, on 11 June 1998. This rather tranquil area, if one can ignore the nearby dual carriageway, once lay in the midst of the Bettisfield colliery. The local station had closed in 1966.

*Pentax 6 x 7    105mm Takumar    Fujichrome 400    1/500, ƒ9.3*

**Fflint station is situated on a section of line that was never quadrupled**, and retains its original Francis Thompson station buildings. In the days when Class 37 locomotives were still a rare sight on the North Wales mainline, No **37431** *Sir Powys / County of Powys*, departs Fflint with the final 1M75 15.00 Cardiff-Rhyl on 13 May 1989. No 37431 emerged as the last ETH conversion from Crewe Works during the 1980s refurbishment program and would face withdrawal in December 1999. *Larry Davies*       *Canon AE1     50mm Canon     Kodachrome 64*

**Connah's Quay Goods Station was situated between Connah's Quay station (closed 1966) and Shotton**, and was the start of the four-track section to Saltney Junction. Only a coal depot remained by the mid 1950s, served by a daily trip from Mold Junction. The photographer was Duty Inspector on Deeside when vandals burned down Connah's Quay No1 signal box. This action led to the closure of the yard in August 1980. In happier times, Class 25 No **25306** passes the signalbox with an 'Up' parcels from Holyhead on 1 April 1980. *Larry Davies* *Canon AE1* *135mm Canon* *Kodachrome 64*

## FOUR TRACK SURVIVOR

**The line through Sandycroft was quadrupled at the turn of the century** and would survive intact until the 1990s. Class 25 No **25278** ambles along the 'up' fast with the 'Warrington Trip' made up of flasks from Wylfa or Trawsfynydd Power Stations,Cargowaggons from Anglesey Aluminium works, cement and domestic oil tanks from Glen Conwy yard, plus assorted empties from Llandudno Junction on 20 September 1985. *Pentax SP1000    200 Pentacon    Ektachrome 100    1/125, f9.3*

**Resplendent in its new eye-catching 'red-band' livery**, Class 31 No **31271** ambles along the 'Up' slow line from Sandycroft with a train of old ballast for the spoil tip at Mold Junction on 4 August 1987. While Freightliner operations exist, the various sections of slow line and loops are a necessary part of the infrastructure to allow freight and passenger trains to co-exist, but this would come to an end in 1991 with closure of the Holyhead Freightliner terminal. *Mamiya 645   80mm Secor C   Ektachrome 100   1/500,f4.5*

'SPENT'
BALLAST

**A gentle breeze carries the sound of a train across the plain towards Sandycroft.** If the signs are correct, it is a heavy train getting away from a signal stop at Mold Junction. The unmistakable outline of a Class 40 begins to take shape and expand rapidly within the confines of my waist-level viewfinder. My thumb trembles on the edge of the shutter-release before it triggers a train of events within the camera, and captures a fraction of the moment on film. Class 40 No **40001**, sounds incredible as it storms past Sandycroft with the 14.40 Lawley Street-Holyhead freightliner train on 27 April 1984. This early pilot-scheme veteran has just three months of activity ahead of it before withdrawal. *Mamiya 645    150mm Secor C    Ektachrome 200    1/500, f6.3*

With four tracks reduced to just two, Mother Nature has moved in to reclaim the land and Curzon Park cutting, Chester, just isn't the same anymore. Resplendent in Large-Logo livery, Class 47 No 47457 Ben Line, is in charge of the down 'Irish Mail' as it speeds through the cutting on 11 June 1988.

*Mamiya 645      110mm Secor C      Ektachrome 100      1/1000, f2.5*

## CHESTER
### CURZON PARK

**The first part of the Chester-Holyhead line to be opened was the section from Chester to Saltney Junction** on 2 November 1846 for the benefit of the Shrewsbury & Chester Railway trains. Class 24 **No 24023**, crosses the Dee Bridge shortly after leaving Chester, with the 13.30 Manchester Victoria-Llandudno on 11 July 1978. The Great Western bridge on the right, erected to coincide with the widening to Saltney Junction, would be extensively renovated in 1979. Thereafter all trains would use this bridge. *Olympus OM1    50mm Zuiko    Ektachrome 200    1/500, f8*

**Class 47 No 47451** heads the 10.04 Holyhead-Euston past the impressive Chester No 2 signal box while a Metro-Cammell Class 101 DMU creeps out of platform 5 with a Cheshire Lines service to Manchester on 23 January 1981. Parliamentary commencement of the Chester & Holyhead Railway Act of 1847 is immediately to the west of this signal box. *Larry Davies* *Canon AE1* *135mm Canon* *Agfachrome*

CHESTER